A VISUAL JOURNEY THROUGH

MAN'S LIFETIME ON EARTH

written by Philip Brooks
illustrated by Kevin Maddison

CONTENTS

INTRODUCTION

This book tells the story of human history from 20,000 BC to today. This is the period during which the species to which we belong, *Homo sapiens*, has been most active on Earth. Some of the events (the evolution of life from the simplest of animals, through the dinosaurs to warm-blooded mammals) that happened *before* 20,000 BC are shown below.

People used to think of history as the lives of the people who ruled us, the wars they fought and the laws they passed. But there are many more interesting happenings – in science and technology, the arts and exploration – that are just as important. So this book covers developments like the invention of the alphabet

and the launch of the first satellite, as well as famous battles and the lives of kings and queens.

Each chapter in the book deals with one historical period. Some periods are longer than others, because sometimes many years went by with few major events. The more recent periods seem packed with fascinating events and there are several reasons for this. The population of the Earth is growing, so more people are doing more things. We also have historical records from more recent periods. And transport has improved, allowing people to communicate with one another and exchange ideas. There is a special foldout section on the story of transport at the end of the book.

EARLY HUMANS

The first people were **nomads**, moving from place to place as they hunted animals and gathered food plants. They made cutting tools from stones and sheltered in caves or huts made from whatever materials they could find. In around 13,000 BC, during the Ice Age, America and Asia were linked by a land bridge and people crossed from Asia to live in North America for the first time.

20,000 BC ▼
Artists in France and Spain painted bulls, deer and other animals on cave walls. These caves may have been the first temples used for **rituals** performed before hunting expeditions.

18,000 BC ▼
People in western Russia built huts using bones of mammoths that had been killed for food.

19,000 BC FLINT TOOLS
Stoneworkers in France learnt how to hammer a piece of flint with another stone to produce very finely worked tools. Flint knives, axes and scrapers were made in this way.

10,000 BC

18,000 BC ▼
With the last Ice Age at its height, temperatures were up to 15°C colder than today.

ASIA

Land bridge

NORTH AMERICA

◀ **16,500** BC
Needles made from pieces of bone, sharpened at one end, were used to sew together animal skins to make clothes.

◀ **10,500** BC
Using local clay, Japanese workers made the first pottery. Pots were soon widely used as all-purpose containers.

10,000 BC ▶
People in western Asia began to settle in villages of round, stone-walled huts.

9

0

AD 2000

THE FIRST FARMERS

About 10,000 BC people began to give up their nomadic way of life and grow food by farming. This happened first in western Asia, in the area of modern Israel and Jordan. They grew **cereal crops** and kept animals. Soon they could produce more food than they needed, and began to trade.

8000 BC ▶
Villagers in western Asia began to build small houses of bricks made of mud dried in the sun.

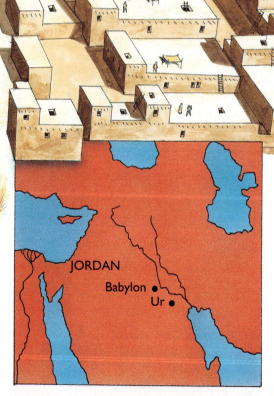

10,000 BC ▲
The first farmers grew emmer, a kind of wheat.

7500 BC

FARM ANIMALS
Sheep and goats were the first farm animals, closely followed by pigs and cattle. These early breeds were smaller than modern ones.

▼ **6500 BC**
Digging sticks were used as farming tools in the sandy soils of western Asia. Soils in China are heavier, so farmers used stone spades.

6000 BC ▼
Traders in the Middle East used stone **seals** to make marks on clay tablets, to identify their property.

◀ **6500 BC**
Deposits of copper were discovered and people learnt how to hammer the metal into shape to make tools and weapons.

THE FIRST CIVILISATIONS

The first cities were built in Mesopotamia (modern Iraq) and Egypt. City dwellers grew rich through trade with nearby towns and villages. They learned skills such as writing and stone building, and developed organised religions.

3500 BC ▼
The Egyptians used rafts of **papyrus** reeds and wooden sailing boats to travel along the river Nile.

3250 BC THE WHEEL
Mesopotamian carpenters built the first wheels.

Made of wooden planks, these early wheels were used on both carts and chariots.

3100 BC ▼
Scribes in the cities of Mesopotamia developed the first writing.

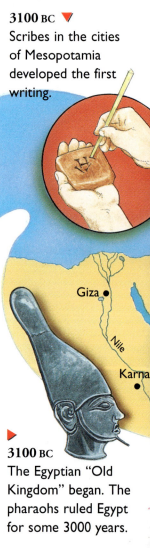

Giza ●

Nile

Karnal ●

▶
3100 BC
The Egyptian "Old Kingdom" began. The pharaohs ruled Egypt for some 3000 years.

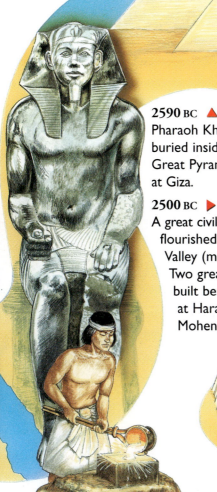

2590 BC ▲
Pharaoh Khufu was
buried inside the
Great Pyramid
at Giza.

2500 BC ▶
A great civilisation
flourished in the Indus
Valley (modern Pakistan).
Two great cities were
built beside the Indus
at Harappa and
Mohenjo-Daro.

3000 BC ▲
Bronze (a mixture of copper
and tin) was used to make tools
and weapons.

2150 BC ▲
A huge **ziggurat** was
built at Ur, Mesopotamia,
as a temple to the moon god.

THE RISE OF EMPIRES

The ancient peoples of the Mediterranean began to try to increase their wealth and influence. Many, like the warlike Hittites and Assyrians, conquered nearby territory. They created huge empires and made the people they ruled pay taxes, called **tribute**, to the emperor. Other peoples, such as the Minoans, increased their riches peacefully, through trade.

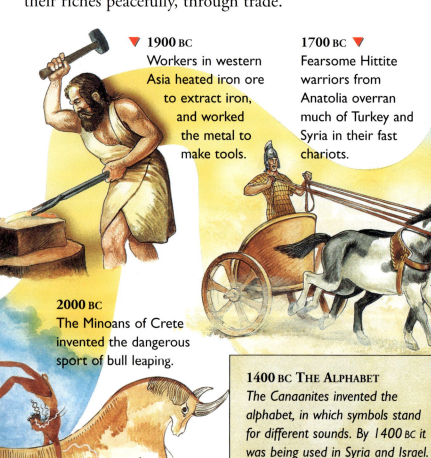

▼ 1900 BC
Workers in western Asia heated iron ore to extract iron, and worked the metal to make tools.

1700 BC ▼
Fearsome Hittite warriors from Anatolia overran much of Turkey and Syria in their fast chariots.

2000 BC
The Minoans of Crete invented the dangerous sport of bull leaping.

1400 BC THE ALPHABET
The Canaanites invented the alphabet, in which symbols stand for different sounds. By 1400 BC it was being used in Syria and Israel. The Phoenicians were another early people to use an alphabet.

10,000 BC

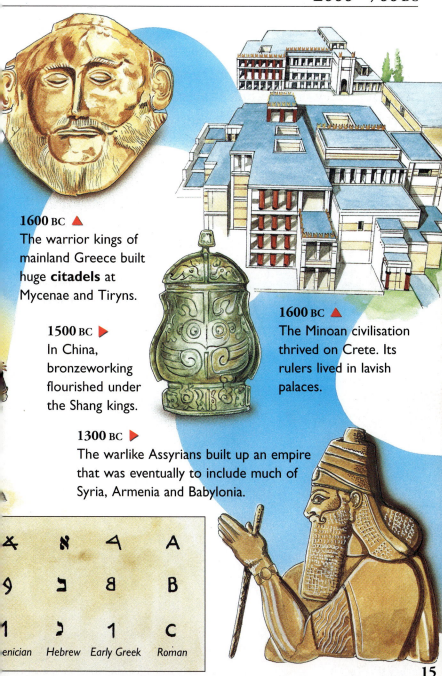

1600 BC ▲
The warrior kings of mainland Greece built huge **citadels** at Mycenae and Tiryns.

1500 BC ▶
In China, bronzeworking flourished under the Shang kings.

1600 BC ▲
The Minoan civilisation thrived on Crete. Its rulers lived in lavish palaces.

1300 BC ▶
The warlike Assyrians built up an empire that was eventually to include much of Syria, Armenia and Babylonia.

𐤀	𐤀	𐤀	A
𐤁	𐤁	𐤁	B
𐤂	𐤂	𐤂	C
enician	Hebrew	Early Greek	Roman

ANCIENT GREECE

At this time Greece was controlled by a number of independent city states. The most powerful were Sparta, a warlike city, and Athens, a trading centre. At the end of the sixth century, they came together to fight the Persian empire, which threatened Greek power from the east. Afterwards, Athens became a great **cultural centre**, producing superb sculpture, architecture and literature.

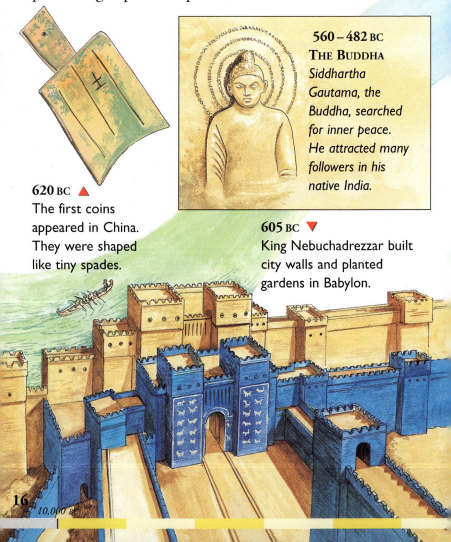

620 BC ▲
The first coins appeared in China. They were shaped like tiny spades.

560 – 482 BC
THE BUDDHA
Siddhartha Gautama, the Buddha, searched for inner peace. He attracted many followers in his native India.

605 BC ▼
King Nebuchadrezzar built city walls and planted gardens in Babylon.

10,000 BC

450 BC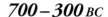
Mediterranean merchants used abacuses to speed up their mathematical calculations.

500 BC
The Greeks built galleys – fast warships with both sails and oars.

438 BC
The Parthenon, a temple to the goddess Athena, was completed in Athens.

423 – 380 BC
The **philosopher** Socrates dominated debates in Athens. His arguments were written down by his pupil, Plato.

0   *AD 2000*

ANCIENT ROME

From small beginnings in Italy, Roman power spread through Europe. By AD117, the Roman empire stretched from Spain to the Persian Gulf, and from England to North Africa. The Romans built many cities, connected them with new, straight roads and kept down rebellions with a large army.

290 BC ▼
The Romans began to increase their power by taking over central Italy.

214 BC ▶
The Emperor of China built the Great Wall of China to keep out northern invaders.

Gaul (France)

Hispania (Spain)

Rome ●

273–238 BC ▲
The Emperor Asoka brought the whole of India under one ruler for the first time.

◀ **70 – 19** BC
The Roman
poet Virgil
wrote the
Aeneid, a
poem about
the hero
Aeneas.

AD **100**
ROMAN BUILDING
*The Romans were the
first to use concrete
on a large scale. They
also developed arches
and vaults (arches
joined together), and
their houses had
underfloor heating.*

4 BC – AD **33** ▲
Jesus Christ was alive in
Palestine. After his **crucifixion**,
followers began to spread
Christianity round
the Roman world.

AD **80** ▶
The Colosseum,
a vast amphitheatre
in Rome,
was completed.
Gladiatorial fights
were staged inside.

RISE OF CHRISTIANITY

In the years after Jesus Christ died there were few Christians because they were punished by the Roman emperors. But when the Emperor Constantine announced that he would **tolerate** Christians, the religion spread quickly. By 400, even people as far south as Aksum, Ethiopia, had converted to Christianity.

150 ▼
Realistic bronze sculpture was developed under the Han dynasty in China.

300 ▲
A city of some 120,000 people was built at Teotihuacan, Mexico. In the centre were huge pyramid temples.

◀ 250
Chinese carpenters built wheelbarrows which could carry loads of up to 150 kilograms.

320 ▶
The Gupta emperors ruled India. They founded new universities, and literature and the arts flourished.

324 ▶
Constantine became Emperor of Rome. He was converted to the Christian religion.

400

HOPEWELL PEOPLE
These people lived in Mississippi, America. They built big burial mounds and left offerings like this stone hand.

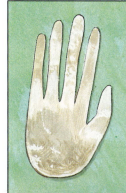

400 ▲
In the Aksum empire of Ethiopia tall stone **obelisks** were built as royal monuments.

NEW EMPIRES

Religion played an important part in two of the empires that came to power in this period. The Christian Byzantine empire, based in Turkey, sprang from the remains of the eastern wing of the Roman empire after the fall of Rome. Meanwhile, a powerful new Muslim empire grew up in the Middle East. Both empires were long-lasting, but the Muslims eventually conquered the Byzantine empire in 1453.

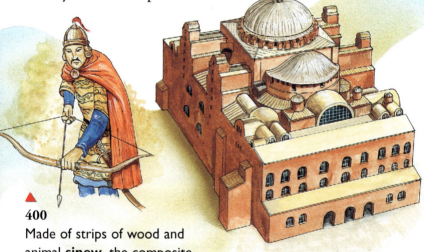

400
Made of strips of wood and animal **sinew**, the composite bow was a fearsome weapon in central Asia.

◀ **410**
Visigoths from eastern Europe invaded Rome. They wrecked the city and destroyed the Roman empire.

537 ▲
The Emperor Justinian ruled the Byzantine empire from Constantinople (modern Istanbul). Here he built the great church of Hagia Sophia. It is roofed with one of the world's largest domes.

10,000 BC

570 – 632
MOHAMMED
The religion of Islam was revealed to its prophet Mohammed. His followers, known as Muslims, spread the faith across the Middle East, founding an Islamic empire.

607
Buddhist temples were built at Nara, Japan.

689 ▼
The Dome of the Rock, Jerusalem, was built on the site where Mohammed is said to have stopped on his journey to heaven.

618
The world's first paper money was produced in China. The idea came from paper receipts given by traders.

INVADERS AND EMPIRES

The eighth and ninth centuries were times of turmoil, especially in Europe. The Frankish empire under Charlemagne expanded quickly across the whole continent before breaking up. At the end of the period, Vikings, forced out of their native Scandinavia by the search for food and land, traded and raided along the European coasts. Meanwhile the powerful Maya were supreme in Central America.

800 ▼

Charlemagne, the king of the Franks (from northern France and Germany) was crowned Emperor of the West. His empire stretched from Denmark to northern Italy. At his capital city, Aachen, he built a large palace and a richly decorated sixteen-sided imperial chapel.

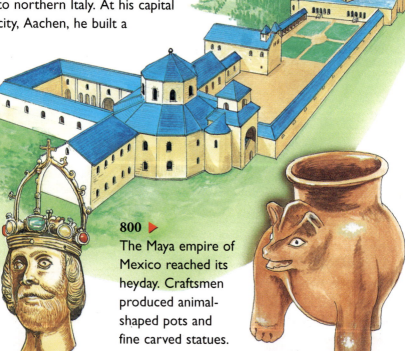

800 ▶
The Maya empire of Mexico reached its heyday. Craftsmen produced animal-shaped pots and fine carved statues.

10,000 BC

◀ **802**
The Khmer empire was founded in Cambodia, southeast Asia. Stone temples were built for the worship of god-kings.

834 ▲
A new tool, the crank, was developed in the Netherlands.

1000
ISLAMIC MEDICINE
Muslim writers, such as the Persian philosopher Avicenna, produced books about medicine. They explained the use of herbs to cure diseases and translated ancient Roman medical textbooks.

850 – 1000 ▲
Viking sailors raided the coasts of Europe and settled in England and France.

York • • Novgorod

851 ▶
Porcelain, a delicate, white form of pottery, was made for the first time in China.

MONKS AND SOLDIERS

In the early Middle Ages the church had great power in Europe, and many cathedrals and monasteries were built. Priests were well educated and did a range of jobs, from teaching and healing the sick to advising kings. The Pope even encouraged Christians to fight the Muslims in Crusades in the Middle East.

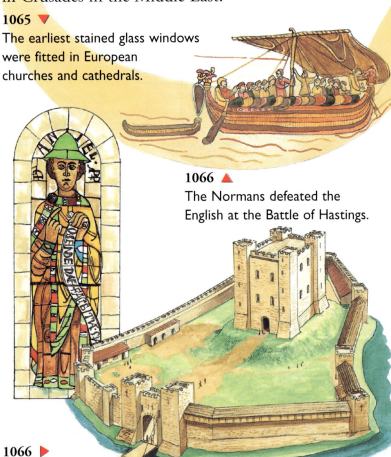

1065 ▼
The earliest stained glass windows were fitted in European churches and cathedrals.

1066 ▲
The Normans defeated the English at the Battle of Hastings.

1066 ▶
England's new Norman rulers built castles all over the country. Each castle was the home of a lord, who kept law and order in his local area.

◀ **1090**
Sailors in China
and the Arab
world used the
magnetic compass
for **navigation**.

1088 ▲
Chinese inventor
Su Sung built a
chiming clock
powered by a large
water wheel.

◀ **1096**
Groups of warriors
from western
Europe set out on
the First Crusade, a
military **campaign**
to conquer
Jerusalem and other
holy places in the
Middle East.

Constantinople

Mediterranean Sea

**Routes of the
first Crusaders**

1187 ▶
The Muslim
warrior Saladin
recaptured
Jerusalem from
the Crusaders.

1206 ▲
The great Mongol
leader Genghis Khan
founded his huge
empire in central
Asia.

WAR AND DISEASE

The Mongols ruled most of Asia after 1200. They opened up trade routes between Europe and Asia. This made it possible for travellers from Europe to get to China for the first time, bringing Chinese silk to European markets. But the trade routes also allowed deadly **plague** germs to travel, killing nearly half the population of Europe.

1300 ▶
Huge stone statues were erected on Easter Island in Polynesia. They probably represent **ancestor** spirits.

Venice

Beijing ●
CHINA

1271 ▲
Marco Polo, from Venice, Italy, was one of the first Europeans to travel over land to China.

1280 ▶
European mechanical clocks had bells to strike the hour, but no dials.

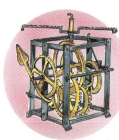

10,000 BC

1300 ▲
Gunpowder, originally
invented in China, was used
in European warfare.

1346 ▲
The Hundred Years' War broke
out between England and France.
It continued on and off until 1453.

1347 ▶
Millions died as the Black Death (bubonic
plague) swept across Europe.

◀ **1362**
China began
a period of
prosperity
under the
Ming dynasty.

1381 ▶
English peasants rebelled when King
Richard II introduced a new **poll tax**.
The king abandoned the tax, but the
leader of the revolt, Wat Tyler, was
killed when fighting broke out.

0   *AD 2000*

NEW DISCOVERIES

The fifteenth century was a time of change all over the world. While large empires were springing up in America and Africa, the new art of the **Renaissance** and the invention of printing were having enormous impact in Europe. For the first time books did not have to be copied out by hand. This made information more widely available and allowed new ideas to spread far more quickly than before.

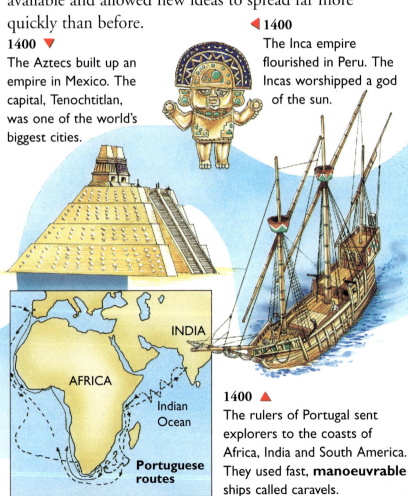

1400 ▼

The Aztecs built up an empire in Mexico. The capital, Tenochtitlan, was one of the world's biggest cities.

◀ **1400**

The Inca empire flourished in Peru. The Incas worshipped a god of the sun.

INDIA

AFRICA

Indian Ocean

Portuguese routes

1400 ▲

The rulers of Portugal sent explorers to the coasts of Africa, India and South America. They used fast, **manoeuvrable** ships called caravels.

10,000 BC

1400s THE RENAISSANCE
A new movement in art started in the cities of Italy. Artists, inspired by the ancient Greeks and Romans, strived for a new realism and placed a new importance on human life and achievements.

1450 ▶
The trading empire of Zimbabwe, Africa, was based in a city with strong, stone walls.

1470 ▲
The astrolabe, used in navigation to work out the altitudes of stars, was developed.

1455 ▶
Johannes Gutenberg of Mainz, Germany, printed the first book using movable type.

31

THE RENAISSANCE SPREADS

As the Renaissance spread to northern Europe, the arts flourished in countries such as England. Meanwhile, a religious revolution began in Germany. Leaders such as Martin Luther and John Calvin criticised corruption in the Catholic church and new, Protestant churches were founded. Protestantism was strong in northern Europe, but weak in the south. Catholic Spain increased in power, with conquests in America, but failed in its plans to take over England.

1543 ▶
Nicolaus Copernicus, a Polish astronomer, published his theory that the Earth orbits the sun.

Earth

Sun

1512 ▲
Michelangelo finished painting the ceiling of the Sistine Chapel in the Vatican, Rome.

◀ **1532**
A group of Spanish knights, led by Francisco Pizarro, conquered the Inca empire of Peru. They took home huge quantities of gold and silver.

◀ **1517**
Religious leader Martin Luther began the Protestant reformation.

1556 ▲
Akbar became Moghul
Emperor of India and
reformed the government.

1558 ▲
The Protestant Elizabeth I
became Queen of England.

◄ **1559**
Philip of Spain
built the Escorial,
a huge monastery-
palace in Madrid.

1590 ▼
In England William Shakespeare
started to work in the
theatre and wrote his
first plays.

1569 ▲
Gerardus Mercator produced the
first modern atlas, based on his new
way of drawing a map of the world.

RELIGIOUS DISPUTES

The beginning of the seventeenth century saw many religious tensions in Europe. Some Protestants left Europe to start new lives in North America where they were free to worship as they pleased. In central Europe, there was a conflict between the Catholic Hapsburg emperors and the Protestant states in their empire. This resulted in the Thirty Years' War. The English Civil War also had a religious aspect, with a Catholic-supporting king opposing a Protestant parliament.

1600 ▼

After a civil war in Japan, the Tokugawa period began. Japan cut itself off from the West under the rule of the Tokugawa **shoguns**.

1600 – 1614 ▼

England, the Netherlands and France started 'East India Companies' to control trade with India and the Far East.

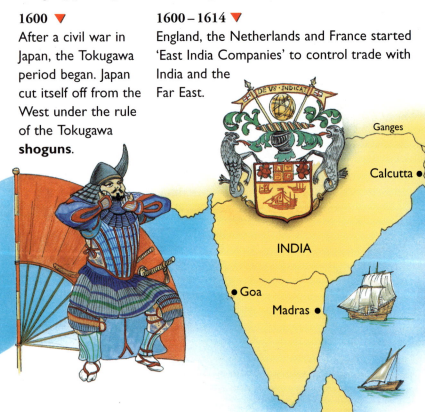

Ganges

Calcutta ●

INDIA

● Goa

Madras ●

1620 ▼

The pilgrims, some of the first English settlers, sailed to America on board the *Mayflower*.

1642 ▼

Frenchman Blaise Pascal made the first mechanical calculator for adding and subtracting.

1632 ▼

Indian Emperor Shah Jahan built the Taj Mahal at Agra as a tomb for his beloved wife Mumtaz Mahal.

1618 – 1638 ▲

The Thirty Years' War broke out between Catholic and Protestant powers in Europe.

1642 ▲

The English Civil War began. Monarchist 'cavaliers' fought parliamentarian 'roundheads'.

ABSOLUTE RULERS

By 1660 Louis XIV (1643–1715) was well established on the French throne. He believed in the divine right of kings–in other words, he ruled as God's representative on Earth. This gave him complete power over his people and an excuse for extravagance, as shown by his vast palace, Versailles. Other rulers at this time, such as Russia's Peter the Great, also tried to wield **absolute** power and reduce the authority of nobles and ministers.

1679 ▶
Frenchman Denis Papin made the first pressure cooker. Food cooks quickly inside the high pressure container.

St Petersburg ●

1675 ▲
St Paul's Cathedral, London, had been damaged in the Great Fire of 1666 which swept through the city. It was rebuilt to new designs by architect Sir Christopher Wren.

1685 ▲

Isaac Newton published his Universal Law of Gravitation. His researches into **gravity**, light and mathematics transformed scientific thinking.

1698 ▶

English engineer Thomas Savery designed a pump to remove water from coal mines. It formed the basis of the steam engine.

SIA

1682
Peter the Great ruled Russia along the lines of a western European power.

1713
Frederick William became King of Prussia. He strengthened the army and reformed the government.

1701 ▼
Jethro Tull's seed drill made seed sowing easier and more efficient.

THE AGE OF REASON

In the early eighteenth century French thinkers used reasoned arguments to challenge ideas like the divine right of kings. The writers of this 'age of reason' championed ordinary people and said that the consent of the people is needed for government to function properly. This was also a great age of technology, with inventions like John Kay's flying shuttle mechanising the cloth industry and bringing about the **Industrial Revolution**.

1726 ▼
Jonathan Swift published the **satire** *Gulliver's Travels.*

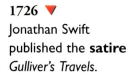

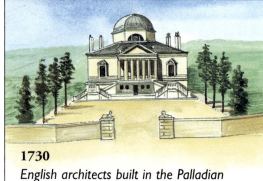

1730
English architects built in the Palladian style, imitating the Italian designer Palladio.

1733 ▶
The Industrial Revolution began in the cloth industry of northern England.

1755
A massive earthquake destroyed two-thirds of the city of Lisbon, Portugal.

1759 ▼
British forces defeated the French in Quebec, giving them control of Canada.

ENCYCLOPEDIE,
DICTIONNAIRE RAISONNÈ
DES SCIENCES,
DES ARTS ET DES MÉTIERS.

TOME PREMIER.

A PARIS,

1750 ▲
Farmer Robert Bakewell developed scientific animal breeding methods.

1751 ▲
In France, Denis Diderot compiled the first encyclopedia.

1752 ▶
American scientist Benjamin Franklin showed that lightning is a form of electricity and invented the lightning conductor.

1757 ▶
A victory at the battle of Plassey brought the region of Bengal, India under British control.

0

THE AMERICAN REVOLUTION

In the 1760s the people of North America began to oppose taxes collected by their rulers in Britain. Protesters in Boston threw tea chests into Boston Harbour in 1773 to show their disapproval of the tax on tea. Soon, Britain and the North Americans were at war and, by 1783, the Americans had won. In Europe, many improvements to machinery pushed forward the rise of industry.

1762
Catherine the Great became Empress of Russia. She promoted industry and encouraged the development of education, especially for women.

1761 ▲
Austrian composer Josef Haydn became music director for the nobleman Prince Esterhazy. He began to write a series of 104 **symphonies**.

1764 ▲
Eight year old composer Wolfgang Amadeus Mozart wrote his first symphony.

1767 ▲
The spinning machine, made by British engineer Joseph Arkwright, was one of several new devices that transformed the textile industry.

1773
The world's first iron bridge was built over the river Severn at Coalbrookdale, England.

1775 ▶
The American Revolutionary War began with the battle of Lexington.

1783 ▲
The Montgolfier brothers from France made the first hot air balloon. After sending up animals, they made the first human flight through the sky above Paris.

1782 ▶
British engineer James Watt made improvements to the steam engine to make it more efficient. It became the main power source for factories.

THE FRENCH REVOLUTION

Many people in France disliked the great power of King Louis XVI. Groups of them started to rebel, forcing the king to make changes and eventually abolish the **monarchy** altogether. For a while, France was a republic, but the military leader Napoleon Bonaparte became so powerful that, in 1804, he was able to crown himself emperor. In a series of wars, Napoleon conquered most of Europe in the early nineteenth century.

1789 ▼

The Bastille prison in Paris, symbol of the king's power, was stormed and captured. This was the start of the French Revolution.

1791 ▲
Toussaint-Louverture led a rebellion of slaves on the island of Haiti.

1790

Writers, including Goethe, Wordsworth and Coleridge, founded the Romantic movement — a new style in art and literature. Romanticism highlights the feelings and emotions of individuals.

1792 ▲
The French leader Napoleon tried to conquer much of Europe. He had victories in Spain, Austria and Prussia, but failed against Britain and Russia.

10,000 BC

◀ **1800**

The first battery was made by the Italian Alessandro Volta. It was made of a pile of zinc plates and pads of fabric moistened with weak acid. The electrical unit, the volt, is named after Volta.

1803

Engineer Richard Trevithick built the first steam engine to run on rails. It went very slowly and was too heavy for its track.

1814 ▲

French doctor René Laënnec made the first simple **stethoscope** to listen to his patients' hearts and lungs.

◀ **1812**

Methods of preserving food by canning were pioneered in France. To begin with, the main customer for canned food was the French army.

THE COMING OF INDUSTRY

Industry spread still more rapidly, and inventions such as the electric motor and photography marked the beginning of modern civilisation. The **political map** of the world was also being redrawn, with revolutionary movements bringing independence for the countries of South America, most of which had been ruled by Spain and Portugal. There were many revolutions in Europe in 1848, although these did not have such a lasting effect.

1821 ▶
During his experiments on electricity and **magnetism**, British scientist Michael Faraday invented the electric motor.

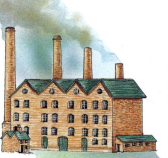

1820s ▲
Many manufacturers took up the steam engine to power factories, the mining industry expanded to provide fuel, and railways and canals were built for transport. As a result industry spread quickly in England, and many people moved to the towns to find work.

1821
The Greeks rebelled against their Turkish rulers. A war began, and the Greeks, supported by Britain, Russia and France, won their freedom in 1829.

 1825
The new state of
Bolivia was named after
Simon Bolivar, who
led South America
to independence
from Spain.

1826
*For the first time a
permanent
photograph was
made using a
metal plate
coated with
light-sensitive
material. The
photographer was
Frenchman Joseph
Nicéphore Niepce.*

1823 ▲
German composer
Ludwig van Beethoven
completed his *Missa
Solemnis*, a setting of
the Catholic mass.
Beethoven's large scale
choral works opened
up new possibilities
in music.

1837
The electric telegraph was
developed to send signals along
a wire. Its inventors were WF
Cooke and Charles Wheatstone.

1840 ▲
Work started on rebuilding
London's Houses of Parliament
after a fire. The building was
finished some 28 years later.

45

NEW NATIONS

In the 1860s and 1870s, two areas made up of many small states, Italy and Germany, became united nations for the first time. But the USA became disunited for a while, with a Civil War that pitted northern against southern states with much loss of life. The north claimed victory in 1865 and immediately abolished slavery. It was the first modern war – railways were used for transport and telegraphs for communication. In fact, many inventions that are now part of modern life first appeared in this period.

1859
After research voyages in his ship, *The Beagle*, Charles Darwin explained the theory of **evolution** in his book *The Origin of Species*.

1856 ▶
The first **internal combustion engine** was designed in France. Its fuel was gas, and it drove factory machinery.

1851 ▼
London's Great Exhibition was housed in the Crystal Palace, a vast building made of iron and glass.

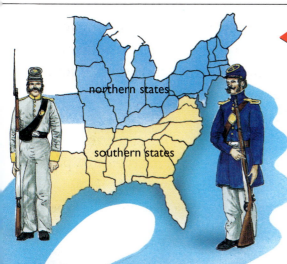

northern states

southern states

◀ **1861**
The American Civil War began. The industrial northern states (whose people wanted to **abolish** slavery) fought the states of the south, where slaves still provided much of the labour on the farms and **plantations**.

◀ **1862**
Scientist Alexander Parkes produced Parkesine, the first plastic.

1874 ▲
A vast new opera house was completed in Paris. One of the world's largest theatres, it seats over two thousand people.

1865 ▲
Surgeon Joseph Lister used **antiseptics** to cut down infection.

1871 ▲
The separate states of Germany united under Chancellor Bismarck.

0

AD 2000

COLONIAL MOVEMENTS

The late nineteenth century saw Europe build up its influence all over the world. Countries like France, Britain and Germany carved up Africa between themselves; the British ruled India and a vast worldwide empire; European countries also tried to put down roots in China. Many of these European powers used their empires as a source of raw materials for their factories, and as markets to sell the goods they produced. But they also brought benefits, such as education and improved legal systems, to their **colonies**.

1876 ▼
The telephone was invented by Alexander Graham Bell, a scientist working with deaf people.

1884 ▼
The first underground railway was built beneath the streets of London.

1884 ▲
Chicago's Home Insurance Building, with its metal framework, was the world's first skyscraper.

◀ **1879**
The electric light bulb was invented. It was soon to light up New York.

1889 ▶
Engineer Gustave Eiffel built his great iron tower in Paris.

1886 ▲
The Statue of Liberty was erected on an island near the entrance to New York's harbour.

1885
Carl Benz built the first motor car. It had a petrol engine and travelled at less than ten miles per hour.

▲
1899
A group of rebels, called the Boxers, started a revolt against foreign power in China. The rising was put down with European help.

49

0   *AD 2000*

WORLD WAR I

In June 1914 Gavrilo Princip, a Serbian, killed Archduke Ferdinand, heir to the throne of Austria. The Austrians blamed Serbia and the two nations were quickly at war. Other European nations were quickly drawn into the war because of the various **alliances** that they had made. Germany, Austria, Hungary, Bulgaria and the Ottoman empire (the Central Powers) fought Britain, France, Italy, Russia and Serbia (the Allies). The war lasted from 1914 to 1918. Some ten million people were killed before the Central Powers were defeated.

1908 ▼

The AEG Factory, one of the first steel and glass buildings, was built in Berlin.

1905 ▼

American brothers Orville and Wilbur Wright built the first successful powered aircraft and made their first flights.

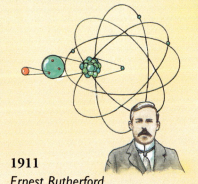

1911
Ernest Rutherford, a scientist from New Zealand, worked out the structure of the atom, the tiniest building block of all the matter in the universe.

10,000 BC

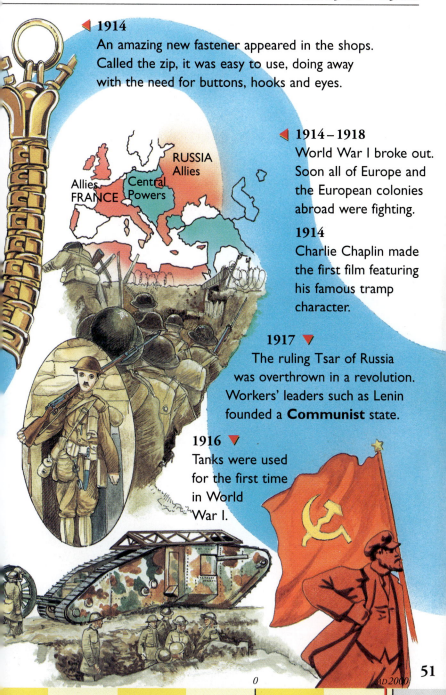

◀ **1914**
An amazing new fastener appeared in the shops.
Called the zip, it was easy to use, doing away
with the need for buttons, hooks and eyes.

RUSSIA
Allies

Allies
FRANCE

Central
Powers

◀ **1914 – 1918**
World War I broke out.
Soon all of Europe and
the European colonies
abroad were fighting.

1914
Charlie Chaplin made
the first film featuring
his famous tramp
character.

1917 ▼
The ruling Tsar of Russia
was overthrown in a revolution.
Workers' leaders such as Lenin
founded a **Communist** state.

1916 ▼
Tanks were used
for the first time
in World
War I.

51

WORLD CRISES

People looked forward to peace after World War I. But other problems soon emerged. Mass unemployment, a stock market crash and widespread poverty ruined the lives of many. In some countries, people turned to strong governments, who tended to deal with poverty but ignore **democracy**. **Fascist** dictators Mussolini in Italy and Hitler in Germany removed opponents violently and began to build up empires. When Italy invaded Ethiopia in 1935 and Germany took over part of Czechoslovakia, it looked as if there would be another war.

1922 ▼
Benito Mussolini was made Prime Minister of Italy. He would soon be a dictator with supreme power over his country.

1924 ▼
Josef Stalin became leader of the Soviet Union (Russia). In four years he was to hold supreme power.

1924
Clarence Birdseye developed the fast freezing process to preserve a range of different foods.

1926 ▶
The value of shares plummeted on the American stock exchange (Wall Street). Many people lost all their money.

◄ **1931**
The Empire State Building, New York, was completed. At that time it was the world's tallest building.

◄ **1933**
The Hoover Dam was begun. It was one of many schemes to produce electricity and to bring work to the USA.

1933
Adolf Hitler was chancellor of Germany. He brought wealth to Germany, but his opponents lost their jobs – or their lives.

1939 ▲
The first successful helicopter was made by engineer Igor Sikorsky.

1928 ▲
Alexander Fleming discovered penicillin, a mould that can kill bacteria.

1936 ▶
Civil War broke out in Spain between Fascists and those who wanted a democratic republic.

0   *AD 2000*

WORLD WAR II

In the 1930s Germany was led by Adolf Hitler. He wanted to expand Germany's borders and took over Czechoslovakia in 1938. Then in 1939 he invaded Poland. Britain and France decided to come to Poland's aid and soon, most of the world was at war. Italy, and later Japan joined Germany's side to form the **Axis** powers. The Axis forces defeated much of Europe, but Britain and the **USSR** (Russia) fought back. Later, the USA entered the war, fighting Japan in the Pacific. The war was not over until the Axis powers were defeated in 1945.

1939 ▼
Germany invaded Poland. Britain and France declared war on Germany.

1941
Japanese aircraft bombed the US naval base at Pearl Harbor, Hawaii. Twenty ships were destroyed and the USA entered the war.

1939 ▲
The first jet aircraft were built.

1942
Enrico Fermi was Italian, but became an American before the Second World War. He directed the first controlled nuclear reaction, on which present-day nuclear reactors are based.

1942 ▶
Rocket-powered **missiles**, built in Germany, were launched on many Allied targets.

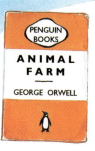

1945 ▲
George Orwell's famous satire, *Animal Farm*, was published.

1945 ▲
The Axis powers surrendered in Europe. After atomic bombs were dropped on Japan, the Japanese also surrendered. During the war more than 50 million people died.

THE POST WAR WORLD

After the end of World War II the two largest world powers were the USSR (Russia) and the USA. These two "superpowers" struggled against each other to dominate the world. They pointed missiles at each other, and supported opposite sides in wars like Vietnam. But they did not actually fight each other. This state of affairs was known as the "cold war". The superpowers also tried to beat each other scientifically. The USSR was the first to get a man into space, but the first men to land on the moon were Americans.

1953 ▼

British scientists worked out the structure of DNA, the substance that carries the **genes** in all living things.

1945 ▲

Many countries of the world joined together to form the United Nations (UN) to encourage world peace. More and more nations joined the UN.

1957
*The Russians launched Sputnik I, a small metal ball that orbited the Earth as the world's first **satellite**.*

1960
Government buildings were opened in Brasilia, the new purpose-built capital of Brazil.

1957 ▲
American singers like Elvis Presley made rock and roll music popular.

1963 ▶
Martin Luther King spoke in support of the rights of black people in the USA.

1969 ▼
Neil Armstrong, an astronaut from the USA, became the first man to step onto the surface of the moon.

◀
1965 – 75
South Vietnam (supported by the USA) was at war with Communist North Vietnam. More than two million people, including many Americans, were killed and the North Vietnamese took over the whole country.

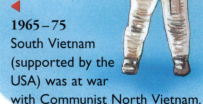

57

THE MODERN WORLD

In the late 1980s the cold war came to an end. Many countries, such as Czechoslovakia and East Germany, threw out their Communist governments. They could elect leaders from any political party for the first time since World War II. The giant USSR broke up, so that small nations like Lithuania and Latvia could be independent. This meant more freedom for many people. But it also brought problems out into the open, as Russian factories with worn-out machinery tried to compete.

1981 ▶
The American space shuttle was launched for the first time. It was the first spacecraft that could be used for more than one mission.

1973 ▼
The opera house at Sydney, Australia, was opened. Its white, sail-like roofs are a striking feature near Sydney harbour.

1984 ▶
New York's AT&T building was completed. With its unusual curving top it began a new style of architecture called Postmodernism.

◀ **1990s**
CD-ROMs began to appear. They carry words, pictures, movies and sound on a disk that can be used in a computer.

1989 ▲
Communist governments fell in Poland, Hungary, Czechoslovakia, East Germany, Romania and Bulgaria.

1991 ▶
After Iraq invaded Kuwait, western powers responded by defeating Iraq in the Gulf War.

1994 ▶
After the campaigns of Nelson Mandela and the African National Congress, free elections took place in South Africa. Black people were given basic human rights for the first time.

▶
1994
The Channel Tunnel between Britain and France was opened.
1996
A probe from the US spacecraft *Galileo* entered the planet Jupiter's atmosphere.

GLOSSARY

abolish to do away with

absolute complete; of a monarch, ruling with total power over a nation

alliance agreement between two or more countries

ancestor person from whom a group of people is descended

antiseptics substances used in medicine to prevent infections

Axis the group of countries fighting on the German side in World War II

campaign a series of related activities, such as a number of battles in a war

cereal crops grains such as wheat, oats, and barley, grown by farmers

citadel fortress

colony a number of people living together in a place far from their homeland but keeping links with it

Communist system of government under which farms, factories, etc, are publicly owned

crucifixion a way of putting someone to death by nailing or tying the hands and feet to a wooden cross

cultural centre city or other settlement that forms the headquarters of a civilisation

democracy form of government by the people or by individuals elected to govern on their behalf

evolution gradual change or development

Fascist term describing the extreme right-wing political party led by Benito Mussolini in Italy between 1922 and 1943, or a similar political movement

gene part of living tissue that contains information about features that are inherited from a person's parents

gladiatorial term used to describe the activities of gladiators, men who fought in Roman arenas to provide entertainment

gravity force by which objects are attracted towards a star or planet

Industrial Revolution a series of changes that brought about the coming of factories and industry in the eighteenth and nineteenth centuries

internal combustion engine which takes its power from a process of burning that takes place within the engine itself

magnetism force by which certain items (such as magnets and planets like the Earth) attract iron and steel

manoeuvrable term used to describe a ship, car, or other vehicle that is easy to steer and can change direction quickly

missile any weapon that is thrown or ammunition that is fired, especially a modern, rocket-propelled weapon

monarchy form of government in which a king or queen is head of state

navigation the job of working out the route of a ship and steering the vessel along the planned route

nomads people who live by travelling from place to place looking for food

obelisk tapering stone column built as a memorial, especially in ancient Egypt

papyrus paper-like substance used in the ancient world and produced from the pith of a reed

philosopher person who studies systems of beliefs in a rational way

plague widespread, deadly, contagious disease, especially the bubonic plague spread by fleas carried by rats that devastated Europe during the fourteenth century

plantation type of farm, formerly staffed by slaves, on which crops such as cotton or rubber are grown

political map map showing the boundaries of empires, nations, and other states

poll tax tax based on a standard fee paid by each person in a country

Renaissance renewal of the arts that took place when artists of the fifteenth century began to be interested in the styles of ancient Greece and Rome

ritual religious or similar ceremony carried out in a set way, usually by a group of people

satellite object that travels round a planet or other heavenly body in a regular orbit

satire a type of book, poem or play in which humour is used to expose evil or stupidity

seal device used to stamp a name or mark on an object to show its ownership or on a document to identify its sender

shogun official who ruled on behalf of the emperor in Japan from the twelfth to nineteenth centuries

sinew tissue attaching muscle to bone

stethoscope device used by doctors to listen to sounds inside the body

symphony large-scale musical piece for orchestra, usually in four separate sections or movements

tolerate to permit or put up with

tribute money or goods given to a ruler by conquered people, as a sort of tax

USSR the Union of Soviet Socialist Republics, the Communist state that included Russia, Ukraine, and other parts of Europe and central Asia. It ceased to exist in 1991

ziggurat large temple, made up of several levels linked by steps, built by people of ancient Iraq

INDEX

TRANSPORT THROUGH THE AGES

Egyptian sailing boat,
1500 BC

Ox-cart
1500 BC

Montgolfier balloon, 1780s

Man of war, 1760s

Steam-powered carriage, 1770s

Stage coach, 18th century

67

Lilienthal glider, 1896

Iron-hulled ship, 1830s

Early steamship, 1802

The *Rocket*, early steam locomotive, 1829

Velocipede, 1830s

Penny farthing, 1870s

Safety bicycle, 1886

Benz car, 1885

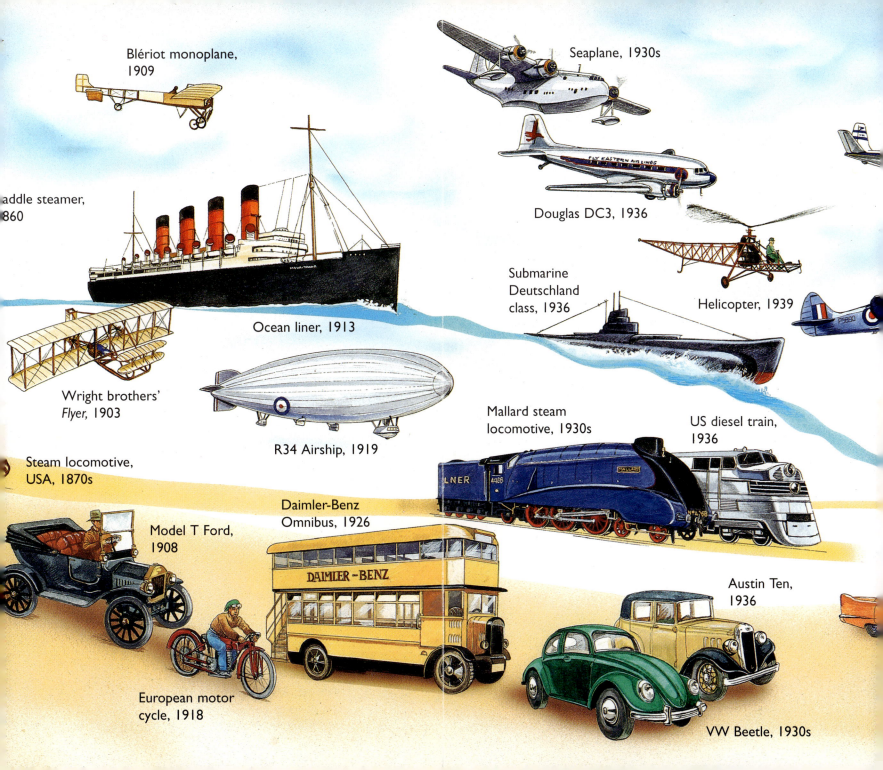

Blériot monoplane, 1909

Seaplane, 1930s

addle steamer, 860

Douglas DC3, 1936

Ocean liner, 1913

Submarine Deutschland class, 1936

Helicopter, 1939

Wright brothers' *Flyer*, 1903

R34 Airship, 1919

Mallard steam locomotive, 1930s

US diesel train, 1936

Steam locomotive, USA, 1870s

Daimler-Benz Omnibus, 1926

Model T Ford, 1908

DAIMLER-BENZ

Austin Ten, 1936

European motor cycle, 1918

VW Beetle, 1930s

Viking longship,
AD 900

Warship of
Henry VIII, early
16th century

Early flying machine,
designed 1488

Greek trireme,
400 BC

Horse-drawn wagon,
16th century